Thank fall

Written by: Ciara L. Hill
Illustrated by: Agia Putri

Thank Fall: A Mindful Story Celebrating the Magic of Autumn

Copyright © 2023 by Ciara L. Hill

All rights reserved. No part of this publication may be reproduced, distributed, or transmitted in any form or by any means, including photocopying, recording, or other electronic or mechanical methods, without the prior written permission of the copyright owner, except in the case of brief quotations embodied in critical reviews and certain other noncommercial uses permitted by copyright law.

Published by:
Lawton Classic Books
Bowie, Maryland 20716

Written by: Ciara L. Hill
Illustrated by: Agia Putri

Printed in the United States of America

ISBN: 978-1-7341565-8-4 (Paperback)
ISBN: 979-8-9884252-0-5 (Hardcover)
ISBN: 979-8-9884252-3-6 (Electronic Book)

Library of Congress Control Number: 2023912031

www.ciaralhillbooks.com

This book belongs to:

Fall was Levi's favorite season. He thought it was the most magical time of year. The leaves changed colors, the days became shorter, and there were plenty of cozy treats and warm drinks. Plus, there were so many holidays that made fall (or autumn, as some people call it), extra special.

Levi loved fall so much that he decided to capture all his favorite things about the season and create a magical autumn potion! He hoped it would remind him of the beauty of fall once the gray skies and cold, icy winter arrived. But first, he had to figure out what to put in it.

One day in late September, Levi asked his mom if he could go on a scavenger hunt around the neighborhood. He needed to find ingredients to add to his autumn potion. He eagerly left as soon as she said it was okay.

The first thing Levi noticed were colorful red, brown, and orange leaves falling from the trees. Then he saw squirrels collecting acorns. "I'm going to add leaves and acorns to my potion," Levi said.

As Levi continued to explore, he could hear the lovely sounds of leaves crunching, birds chirping, and the wind whistling. "I am going to add the crunch of the leaves, the chirp of the birds, and the whistle of the wind to my potion!" Levi said.

Levi then bent down and picked up a bumpy pinecone. It was next to a smooth, plump pumpkin.

"I am going to add the pinecone and pumpkin to my potion," Levi declared.

Then, he smelled something delicious in the air: two pies—one sweet potato and one apple—were cooling on a windowsill. Levi imagined taking a big bite of the tasty treats.

"I am going to add the sweet smells of those pies to my potion," said Levi, trying not to drool.

His next stop was the park, where he saw his friends playing with a football. They were laughing and cheering as they ran around.

"Football is so exciting! I am going to add that fun feeling to my potion," Levi said.

But after he added all the ingredients to the potion, Levi felt like something was still missing. So, he decided to ask his parents for help.

"Mom, Dad, can you help me?" asked Levi. After telling them about his potion, he said, "I am still missing some things that make fall special to me! What else should I add?"

Levi's mother suggested, "You love being around people. Why don't you add something that reminds you of your family and friends?"
"And maybe you can add something that makes you feel good," added Levi's dad. Levi listened carefully and knew his parents' ideas would help him make the best autumn potion ever.

The next day was the fall festival. Levi could not wait to dress up in his costume and join his friends for a day of fun. He took a picture to capture the moment. He loved looking back at photos and thinking about fun memories.

"I can add a photo to my potion," Levi whispered to himself.

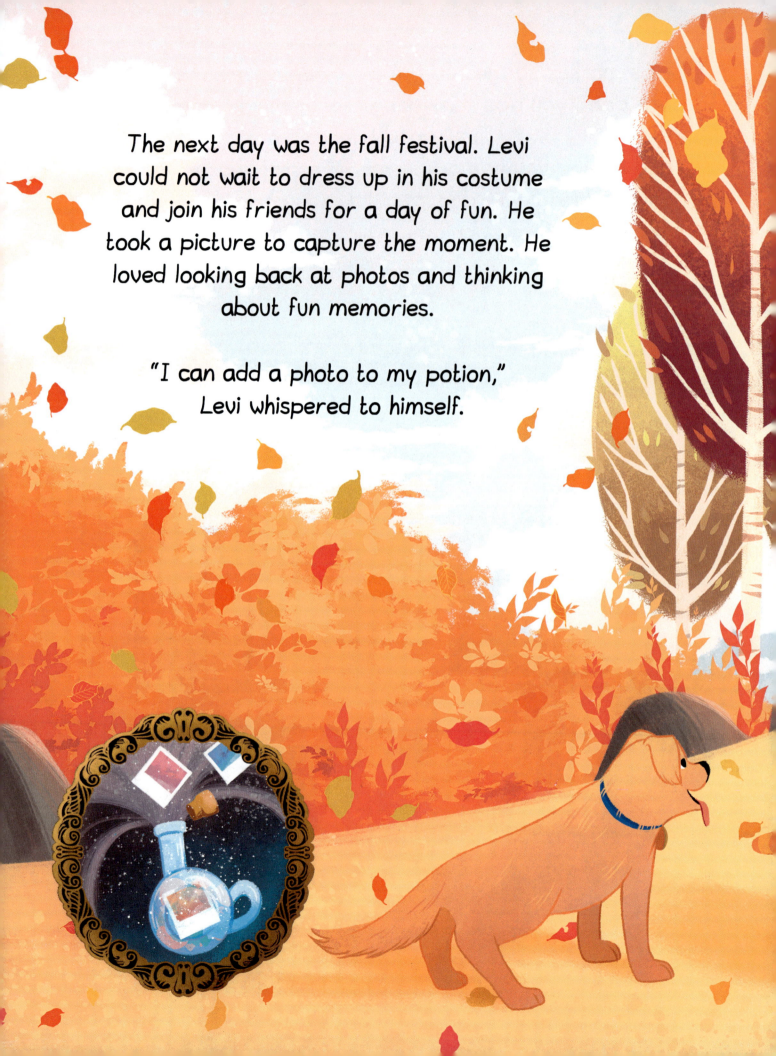

When Levi returned home, his parents played his favorite rhythm and blues music. The sound of his family singing along filled the air, and Levi felt happy as they danced together.

I want to add happiness to my potion, Levi thought.

As the weeks passed, Levi enjoyed more of his favorite fall activities, such as going on hayrides and visiting pumpkin patches. Each adventure brought new memories, but he knew there were still more special things that he wanted to add to his magical autumn potion.

He wasn't sure what they were yet, but he knew the perfect ingredients would come his way.

Finally, on a day in late November, Levi's family gathered to honor, reflect, and celebrate everything they were grateful for. When Levi's grandparents arrived, they gave him a huge hug that made him feel so loved.

"I've got it!" Levi excitedly announced. "I'll add a big hug to my potion!"

Levi could smell all kinds of delightful food in the air. His stomach rumbled, just like it had a few weeks before when he smelled those yummy pies cooling on the windowsill. But this time, Levi could eat what he smelled. And boy, did he eat!

"Yummy food is definitely going into my potion," said Levi.

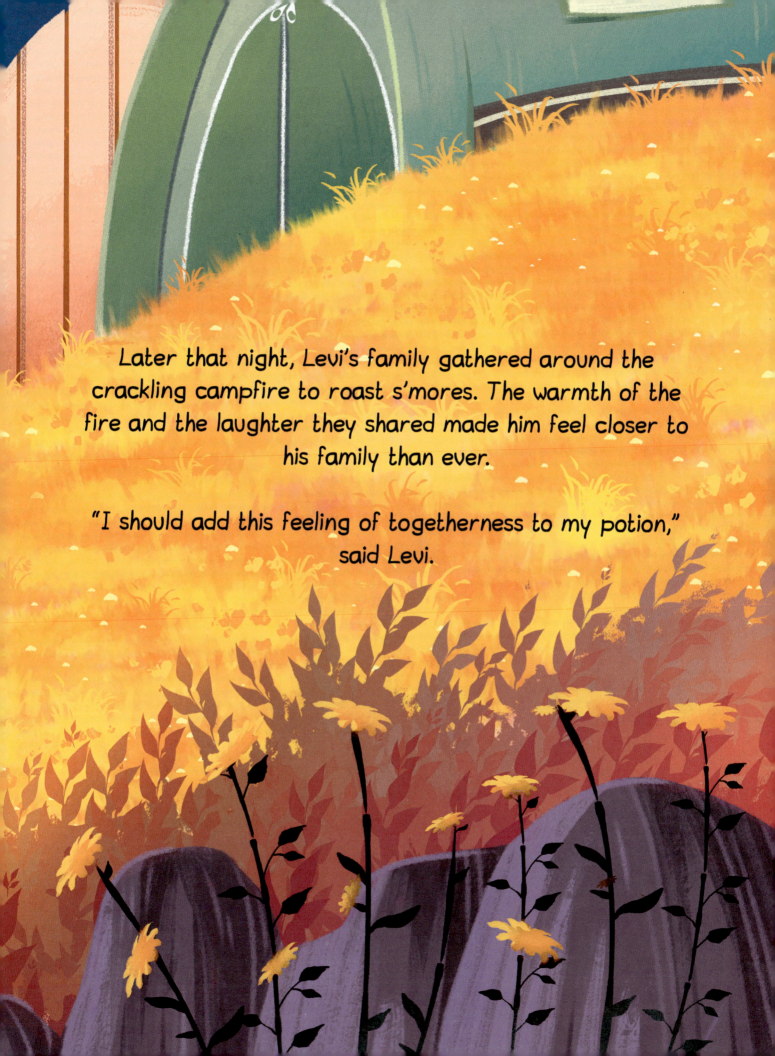

Later that night, Levi's family gathered around the crackling campfire to roast s'mores. The warmth of the fire and the laughter they shared made him feel closer to his family than ever.

"I should add this feeling of togetherness to my potion," said Levi.

And then, Levi realized that his perfect autumn potion was complete! It was a combination of all the things he could see, hear, touch, smell, and taste, along with the things that filled his heart with joy. Levi thanked fall for all the magical things that only happened during this wonderful season.

Levi filled a tiny bottle with his special autumn potion and put it on a necklace. He knew that it would always remind him why fall was indeed the best season of all.

"Fall is really magical," Levi said happily, looking at his necklace. "I can't wait until next year!"

Draw your own autumn potion

Thank you for reading Thank Fall.

I hope you enjoyed it! As an independent author that writes stories focused on positively highlighting inclusive representation in children's books, gaining exposure relies mainly on word-of-mouth. So please leave a review wherever you can.

Downloadable resources for Thank Fall and my other books, Soulful Holidays, Shiloh and Dande the Lion, and Cocoa Mistletoe, can be found at www.ciaralhillbooks.com.

I love picture mail! Share a photo of your family reading Thank Fall, for a chance to be featured on my social media pages! Please email your pictures to ciaralhillbooks@gmail.com.

Made in the USA
Monee, IL
21 September 2023